THE NINE BEATITUDES

THE NINE BEATITUDES

Craig Munro

RITCHIE

John Ritchie Publishing

40 Beansburn, Kilmarnock, Scotland

ISBN-13: 978 1 912522 49 1

Copyright © 2019 by John Ritchie Ltd.
40 Beansburn, Kilmarnock, Scotland

www.ritchiechristianmedia.co.uk

Typeset by John Ritchie Ltd., Kilmarnock
Printed by Bell & Bain Ltd., Glasgow

Contents

Foreword

This is the second of a series that Craig Munro has undertaken, dealing with familiar Bible topics. He first covered *The Ten Commandments* and now he steps down a digit to cover *The Nine Beatitudes.*

When you consider that the Old Testament closes with the threat of a curse (Mal 4.6), it is thrilling that the New Testament virtually opens with these pronouncements of blessing from the Lord Jesus Himself, and skilfully, Craig expounds each of them.

He firmly believes that in the future the Lord Jesus will reign universally; His administration will be a literal kingdom that will span 1000 years. However, that does not preclude the fact that presently, in a spiritual sense, believers are subjects of the kingdom of God's dear Son (Col 1.13). Hence the author does not relate the teaching of the Sermon on the Mount exclusively to those who will believe subsequent to the Church being raptured. He sees the Sermon's moral demands as relevant to the church age, for so they are. Read the epistle by James to discover that to be true.

The book is well worth reading on a number of counts. First, Craig sees the Lord Jesus as being the chief exemplar of the moral qualities that warrant the pronouncement of blessing. Thus, the heart is drawn to Him, as from Old Testament prophecies, New Testament history and apostolic ministry, Craig directs us to our beloved Saviour.

Then there is a note of challenge, as the author probes our consciences as to whether the qualities that the Lord lists feature in our own lives. Number 1; are we poor in spirit or self-assertive? Number nine; are we willing be slandered for His Name's sake or do we go for the easy option? From the first to the last of these Beatitudes Craig incisively applies the Lord's ministry. He holds the plumb line of the Saviour's teaching up against modern attitudes and life choices.

Finally, there is much to cheer us in the book, as we are encouraged to lift up our heads and anticipate the rich recompense that awaits those who do meet the criteria for blessing; "Blessed are…**FOR**", and on nine occasions a reason is furnished as to why spiritual and persecuted souls should be heartened despite difficulties. The fact that future prospects are bright sweetens the believer's experiences of life, even when his outlook and behaviour see him swimming against the tide of current thinking. So read the book, and prepare to be enlightened, challenged and encouraged by it.

Jack Hay

Introduction

This book considers *the beatitudes*, or blessings, given by the Lord Jesus when He commenced preaching the famous "Sermon on the Mount" (Matthew chapters 5 - 7). It contains some of the most famous teachings and sayings of the Lord Jesus and the "Sermon on the Mount" is often referenced in common day speech, even by people with a very limited understanding of the Bible. Perhaps, however, it is an area that is referenced much more than it is read, and certainly it is rarely explained, even amongst true believers.

And yet, these beatitudes are the heart of the message of Christ. His message fundamentally changed character and mindsets. He was not here to gather adherents where mere mental assent to some key beliefs was all that was required. No, the whole life and character of disciples had to be changed and conformed to His standards, the standards of Heaven.

This book is the second published book in a series which tries to deal with a key chapter or section of Scripture. The intention is to publish accessible books on the following key chapters of the Bible:

1. The 10 Commandments - Exodus 20
2. The 9 Beatitudes - Matthew 5
3. The 8 Kingdom Parables - Matthew 13
4. The 7 Feasts of Jehovah - Leviticus 23
5. The 6 Days of Creation - Genesis 1

Each verse, commandment, beatitude, parable, feast, and day will be expounded briefly, and the chapter will be readable in less than five minutes. At the end of each chapter there is a space for notes and personal reflections on the Scriptures

All references and Scripture references will be placed in a footnote. The purpose is to allow each chapter to be read quickly, but to provide scriptural evidence for any interpretations given, to allow readers to explore the subject more fully if they so desire. I strongly encourage the reader to read these Scriptures. It is the Scriptures that carry the power to transform our lives.

Reading, meditating, and obeying the Holy Scriptures are the essential elements of a Christian's life. It is hoped that by providing thoughts on these important sections of Scripture in an accessible and concise manner they may be useful for personal study and reflection and perhaps for group/Bible Class discussion.

The substance of this book was first published in the *Present Truth* magazine. The material has now been edited further and expanded for this current volume. My simple prayer is that through publishing this book, the Lord Jesus may be exalted, and God's people built up in their most holy faith. My burden is for a movement in our day back to the Bible with a deeper reverence and obedience to His Word.

Overview of the Beatitudes

The nine beatitudes were spoken by the Lord Jesus on a hill near Lake Galilee. They are the opening words of the 'Sermon on the Mount' (Matthew chapters 5-7) and are recorded for us in Matthew's Gospel chapter 5 vs 1-10. Some of the beatitudes are also recorded in Luke 6 verses 20-22.

The Lord had some very specific things to say to His own disciples about the principles of living and how to be blessed. He takes them up into a mountain and sits down ('when he was set'), the normal position for teachers to assume when teaching the law. Opening His mouth to ensure complete engagement He then gave the following inspired nine beatitudes. '*And seeing the multitudes, he went up into a mountain: and when he was set, his disciples came unto him: And he opened his mouth, and taught them, saying....*'.

Principles for Living -
How to be Blessed

Beatitude 1
Matthew 5.3 Blessed are the poor in spirit: for theirs is the kingdom of heaven.

eatitude 2

Matthew 5.4 Blessed are they that mourn: for they shall be comforted.

eatitude 3

Matthew 5.5 Blessed are the meek: for they shall inherit the earth.

eatitude 4

Matthew 5.6 Blessed are they which do hunger and thirst after righteousness: for they shall be filled.

eatitude 5

Matthew 5.7 Blessed are the merciful: for they shall obtain mercy.

eatitude 6

Matthew 5.8 Blessed are the pure in heart: for they shall see God.

eatitude 7

Matthew 5.9 Blessed are the peacemakers: for they shall be called the children of God.

eatitude 8

Matthew 5.10 Blessed are they which are persecuted for righteousness' sake: for theirs is the kingdom of heaven.

eatitude 9

Matthew 5.11-12 Blessed are ye, when men shall revile you, and persecute you, and shall say all manner of evil against you falsely, for my sake. Rejoice, and be exceeding glad: for great is your reward in heaven: for so persecuted they the prophets which were before you.

Each of these beatitudes begins with the word which translates to be "happy", or "blessed". The underlying Greek word and the equivalent Latin noun describe a state of blessedness. The Latin word is anglicised to "beatitude". The beatitudes, therefore, describe what the Lord Jesus holds to be blessings and happiness.

Christianity is about a personal relationship with Christ by being born again[1]. It is, of course, centred around His death and resurrection[2], and through faith in Christ[3] Christians enjoy forgiveness of sins[4] and the certain hope of heaven[5]. However, Christianity is also about blessings in the present. It is about the development of Christian character in our lives on earth and the holding dear of all that is good and true.

---

[1]John 3. 3: 'Except a man be born again, he cannot see the kingdom of God.'

[2]1 Corinthians 15. 1-4: 'Moreover, brethren, I declare unto you the gospel which I preached unto you, which also ye have received, and wherein ye stand; By which also ye are saved, if ye keep in memory what I preached unto you, unless ye have believed in vain. For I delivered unto you first of all that which I also received, how that Christ died for our sins according to the scriptures. And that he was buried, and that he rose again the third day according to the scriptures.'

[3]Ephesians 2. 8-9: 'For by grace are ye saved through faith; and that not

This is where the Lord Jesus starts His public teaching with the 'Sermon on the Mount'. From Christ's teaching we learn much about His character and the characteristics He expects to see in His disciples. In the eight parables in Matthew 13 the emphasis will be on the *kingdom of Christ.* In the upper room ministry (John 13 - 17) the emphasis will be on *communion with Christ.* In the Olivet discourse (Matthew 24-25) the emphasis will be on the *coming of Christ.* But the foundation of all His teaching is the development of Christian character. These are the principles that mark His kingdom now and eternally.

of yourselves: it is the gift of God: Not of works, lest any man should boast.'

[4]Ephesians 1. 7: 'In whom we have redemption through his blood, the forgiveness of sins, according to the riches of his grace.'

[5]John 14. 1-3: 'Let not your heart be troubled: ye believe in God, believe also in me. In my Father's house are many mansions: if it were not so, I would have told you. I go to prepare a place for you. And if I go and prepare a place for you, I will come again, and receive you unto myself; that where I am, there ye may be also.'

Characteristics

Each beatitude describes a feature that should mark the believer:

	Blessed are...	or those who are:
1	the poor in spirit	*self-emptied*
2	they that mourn	*sorrowful*
3	the meek	*self-restrained*
4	they which do hunger and thirst after righteousness	*striving for righteousness*
5	the merciful	*sympathetic*
6	the pure in heart	*sanctified*
7	the peacemakers	*serene*
8	they which are persecuted for righteousness' sake	*suffering*
9	ye when men shall revile you, and persecute you, and shall say all manner of evil against you falsely, for my sake	*slandered*

Outcomes

Each beatitude also describes the outcome for the believer if these characteristics are displayed in them.

For....

1	theirs is the kingdom of heaven	*privilege*
2	they shall be comforted	*protection*
3	they shall inherit the earth	*possession*
4	they shall be filled	*provision*
5	they shall obtain mercy	*pitied*
6	they shall see God	*pre-eminence*
7	they shall be called the children of God	*position*
8	theirs is the kingdom of heaven	*privilege*
9	Rejoice, and be exceeding glad: for great is your reward in heaven: for so persecuted they the prophets which were before you	*prize*

$\mathscr{B}$eatitude

Blessed Are The Poor In Spirit:
For Theirs Is The Kingdom Of Heaven.

(Matthew 5.3)

The blessing of
a self-emptied life

$\mathscr{W}$hat must the audience of Israelites have been expecting when the Saviour climbed a mountain in Galilee and commenced His ministry on earth? John had publicly announced Him as the Lamb of God. Others believed Him to be virgin born. Some said that they had heard God speak to Him directly from heaven at the Jordan, others that even as a boy He knew the Scriptures to such an extent that the doctors of the law had been baffled with His insight and questions. Word had spread of Him healing the sick, removing demons from possessed individuals, making the blind to see and the lame walk. People gathered from Syria, Galilee, Decapolis and Jerusalem to hear Him teach. No synagogue could hold the audience and so they climbed the hill after Christ. What would He say? Would He be a political revolutionary who would remove Israel from under the heel of Rome? Would He endorse His religious ideology with some outstanding miracle? Was His message social? What was this new Rabbi's message?

What a shock they would all receive. The Lord Jesus Christ did not conform to anything they may have pre-supposed. They watched Him deliberately sit down, as all teachers did who expounded the

Scriptures authoritatively. He slowly opened His mouth to still the gathered throng that they might hear a solemn and significant utterance. They then heard Him say, "Blessed".

'Blessed are'

His first word was "Blessed".   This word (*makarios*) can be rendered "happy".   The word 'are' is missing in the language which He spoke and so the opening word could be rendered '*O the blessedness of*', or '*O the happiness of*'.   He had come with a message of happiness.   His message was not a call to arms as a new political revolutionary, nor did it resemble the pride of a religious Pharisee or the condemnatory tone of a new prophet. His communication style and content were altogether different.

'the poor in spirit'

Other philosophers of this period had taught that happiness was to be found in honour, riches, splendour, or sensual pleasure. The Lord Jesus was different.   He fixed His eye on the poor and the humble, asserting that happiness was to be found in poverty and not in the pomp and splendours of life.   He had come to bless the humble – especially those who knew their deep spiritual poverty. He is not blessing the poor-spirited – i.e. those who lack vitality and courage.   No! He is not only blessing those who were literally poor and hungry (He would do so.[6]) but more fundamentally He had come to bless those where poverty of soul was a frame of

[6]Luke 6. 20: 'And he lifted up his eyes on his disciples, and said, Blessed be ye poor: for yours is the kingdom of God.'

[7]Luke 10. 21: 'In that hour Jesus rejoiced in spirit, and said, I thank thee, O Father, Lord of heaven and earth, that thou hast hid these things from the wise and prudent, and hast revealed them unto babes: even so, Father; for so it seemed good in thy sight.';

John 11.33: 'When Jesus therefore saw her weeping, and the Jews

mind. It is the place where self-assertiveness and pride are entirely absent, and God is all in all[7]. This self-emptying conviction is the fitting state to receive spiritual blessing[8]. These are the people that the Saviour says are blessed.

He had exhibited this mind-set Himself. He, who was on equality with God, co-equal, co-eternal, *'emptied Himself'[9]*, veiling His glory, and became a man, a servant to His God and Father. He who was *"rich"* became *"poor"*[10]. He who is the Creator of the universe became not only the carpenter of Nazareth but completely dependent upon His Father, God. He never claimed His rights or resisted when His rights were ignored. When He was insulted, He offered no insult in return[11]. He bowed His head to receive a crown of thorns instead of the royal diadem which was His right as King of Kings and Lord of Lords. He taught that true blessedness is known when we move in total dependence on God and self is denied.

The importance of humility in life is a feature of Matthew's Gospel and the Lord would constantly build on this foundation in His teaching. It was He who requested that we *'Come'* to Him and *'take*

also weeping which came with her, he groaned in the spirit, and was troubled.';

1 Peter 2.23: 'Who, when he was reviled, reviled not again; when he suffered, he threatened not; but committed himself to him that judgeth righteously';

1 Peter 5.5: 'Yea, all of you be subject one to another, and be clothed with humility: for God resisteth the proud, and giveth grace to the humble.'

[8] 1 Corinthians 4.6-7: 'And these things, brethren, I have in a figure transferred to myself and to Apollos for your sakes; that ye might learn in us not to think of men above that which is written, that no one of you be puffed up for one against another. For who maketh thee to differ from

His yoke upon us' for He said, *'I am lowly in heart'*[12] He is the King that is to come, *'meek and sitting upon an ass'*[13]. He was born in Bethlehem, *'the least of the princes of Judah'*[14]. The Lord used a child as an illustration to answer the disciples' questions of who should be the greatest[15]. It was He who said that the greatest in the kingdom of heaven was the person that regarded themselves as the least[16] and again, *'those who humble themselves shall be exalted'.*[17]

'for theirs is'

This blessing is not only for the future but to be enjoyed now in the present. The present tense "is" is used in this blessing and not the future tense "will be". This must have perplexed the Jewish audience. In what sense could the future restored Kingdom of Israel be enjoyed right now? Perhaps it dawned on them that even Gentiles could be blessed. This kingdom must be spiritual and eternal and far greater than the national and physical kingdom of a future day. His preaching would give present assurance and **hope** to all who were dependent upon God alone. Our blessing and happiness are not just the security of a future anticipation but a present reality.

another? and what hast thou that thou didst not receive? now if thou didst receive it, why dost thou glory, as if thou hadst not received it?';
Revelation 3.17-18: 'Because thou sayest, I am rich, and increased with goods, and have need of nothing; and knowest not that thou art wretched, and miserable, and poor, and blind, and naked: I counsel thee to buy of me gold tried in the fire, that thou mayest be rich; and white raiment, that thou mayest be clothed, and that the shame of thy nakedness do not appear; and anoint thine eyes with eyesalve, that thou mayest see.';
Matthew 9.12-13: 'But when Jesus heard that, he said unto them, They that be whole need not a physician, but they that are sick. But go ye and learn what that meaneth, I will have mercy, and not sacrifice: for I am not come to call the righteous, but sinners to repentance.'

'the Kingdom of Heaven'

He had come to speak about the kingdom. Of course, He would know that their minds would be concerned with the physical manifestation of that kingdom when Israel's old boundaries would be restored and extended, and peace would reign upon the world in a millennial age[18]. But, here, He is assuring them that the kingdom is already the possession of the poor in spirit. Fellowship with heaven can take place now. The riches of the realm of **heaven** can be enjoyed by those who are cast upon God. We can now enter the blessings of the kingdom. The King has come!

[9]Philippians 2.5-8: 'Let this mind be in you, which was also in Christ Jesus: Who, being in the form of God, thought it not robbery to be equal with God: But made himself of no reputation, (or alternatively 'emptied Himself') and took upon him the form of a servant, and was made in the likeness of men: And being found in fashion as a man, he humbled himself, and became obedient unto death, even the death of the cross'.
This does not mean He emptied Himself of anything. To say He emptied Himself of His deity is blasphemous. No. He emptied Himself, He poured Himself out. The word is used as a figure like a liquid being poured from one vessel of a particular shape to another of a different shape but always remaining the same liquid and the same volume. He was made in the form of a servant but never ceased to be who He always was, God.
[10]2 Cor. 8. 9: 'For ye know the grace of our Lord Jesus Christ, that, though he was rich, yet for your sakes he became poor, that ye through his poverty might be rich.'
[11]1 Peter 2. 22-23: 'Who did no sin, neither was guile found in his mouth: Who, when he was reviled, reviled not again; when he suffered, he threatened not; but committed himself to him that judgeth righteously.'
[12]Matthew 11.29: 'Take my yoke upon you, and learn of me; for I am meek and lowly in heart: and ye shall find rest unto your souls.'

[13]Matthew 21.5: 'Tell ye the daughter of Sion, Behold, thy King cometh unto thee, meek, and sitting upon an ass, and a colt the foal of an ass.'

[14]Matthew 2.6: 'And thou Bethlehem, in the land of Juda, art not the least among the princes of Juda: for out of thee shall come a Governor, that shall rule my people Israel.'

[15]Matthew 18.1-4: 'At the same time came the disciples unto Jesus, saying, Who is the greatest in the kingdom of heaven? And Jesus called a little child unto him, and set him in the midst of them, And said, Verily I say unto you, Except ye be converted, and become as little children, ye shall not enter into the kingdom of heaven. Whosoever therefore shall humble himself as this little child, the same is greatest in the kingdom of heaven.'

[16]Matthew 11.11: 'Verily I say unto you, Among them that are born of women there hath not risen a greater than John the Baptist: notwithstanding he that is least in the kingdom of heaven is greater than he.'

[17]Matthew 23.12: 'And whosoever shall exalt himself shall be abased; and he that shall humble himself shall be exalted.'

[18]Isaiah 65.17-25: 'For, behold, I create new heavens and a new earth: and the former shall not be remembered, nor come into mind. But be ye glad and rejoice for ever in that which I create: for, behold, I create Jerusalem a rejoicing, and her people a joy. And I will rejoice in Jerusalem, and joy in my people: and the voice of weeping shall be no more heard in her, nor the voice of crying. There shall be no more thence an infant of days, nor an old man that hath not filled his days: for the child shall die an hundred years old; but the sinner being an hundred years old shall be accursed. And they shall build houses, and inhabit them; and they shall plant vineyards, and eat the fruit of them. They shall not build, and another inhabit; they shall not plant, and another eat: for as the days of a tree are the days of my people, and mine elect shall long enjoy the work of their hands. They shall not labour in vain, nor bring forth for trouble; for they are the seed of the blessed of the LORD, and their offspring with them. And it shall come to pass, that before they call, I will answer; and while they are yet speaking, I will hear. The wolf and the lamb shall feed together, and the lion shall eat straw like the bullock: and dust shall

be the serpent's meat. They shall not hurt nor destroy in all my holy mountain, saith the LORD.'

Revelation 20.4-6: 'And I saw thrones, and they sat upon them, and judgment was given unto them: and I saw the souls of them that were beheaded for the witness of Jesus, and for the word of God, and which had not worshipped the beast, neither his image, neither had received his mark upon their foreheads, or in their hands; and they lived and reigned with Christ a thousand years. But the rest of the dead lived not again until the thousand years were finished. This is the first resurrection. Blessed and holy is he that hath part in the first resurrection: on such the second death hath no power, but they shall be priests of God and of Christ, and shall reign with him a thousand years.'

Lesson

To have a happy life, I need to empty myself of selfish thoughts and desires and live humbly before God. To what extent is our life one of humility and self-denial?

> He hath shewed thee, O man, what is good; and what doth the LORD require of thee, but to do justly, and to love mercy, and to walk humbly with thy God?
>
> Micah 6.8

Notes

Blessed Are They That Mourn:
For They Shall Be Comforted.

(Matthew 5.4)

The blessings of
the sorrowful

'Blessed are'

The vast crowds that gathered around Christ must have wondered whom He would include in His second blessing on the mountain of beatitudes. They had already been astonished that the Lord had firstly pronounced happiness to the humble and to those who exhibited deep poverty of soul. Who would be next?

'They that mourn'

Blessed are they that mourn! What a shock they would all receive when the Lord singled out the mourner for happiness. This would, of course, include those who had recently been bereaved of a loved one, but it would not be isolated to such a group. Indeed, it would principally include all that were mourning because of conditions in the land, for example, Zacharias and

---

[19]Luke 1.5-6: 'There was in the days of Herod, the king of Judaea, a certain priest named Zacharias, of the course of Abia: and his wife was of the daughters of Aaron, and her name was Elisabeth. And they were both righteous before God, walking in all the commandments and ordinances of the Lord blameless.'

Elizabeth[19],Simeon[20] and Anna[21], John the Baptist[22] and many others like them. Mourners would include those who longed for better days; for true repentance in the hearts of the people; for God to be given His proper place; for holiness to mark the House of God; for righteousness and peace to mark the kingdom, and for the King to return in glory.

Those who longed for better days were in a minority. No doubt some would point out that the House of God had now been built after forty-six years[23], and that the sacrificial system had recommenced after lying dormant for many years. What was there to mourn about? They were happy under the heel of Rome with their sin and their man-made feasts. Complacency is always the scourge of spiritual progress.

There were those, however, whose grief could not be concealed and felt that God deserved far better. The godly have always mourned and called for repentance amongst God's people. Daniel prayed: *'We have sinned'*[24]. Nehemiah prayed: *'We have sinned'*[25]. Our blessed Lord said that special blessing and happiness would be extended to such a people. God always blesses His people when there is heartfelt repentance and dependency upon Him.

[20]Luke 2.25: 'And, behold, there was a man in Jerusalem, whose name was Simeon; and the same man was just and devout, waiting for the consolation of Israel: and the Holy Ghost was upon him.'

[21]Luke 2.36-37: 'And there was one Anna, a prophetess, the daughter of Phanuel, of the tribe of Aser: she was of a great age, and had lived with an husband seven years from her virginity; And she was a widow of about fourscore and four years, which departed not from the temple, but served God with fastings and prayers night and day.'

[22]Luke 3.2-3: '..the word of God came unto John the son of Zacharias in the wilderness. And he came into all the country about Jordan, preaching the baptism of repentance for the remission of sins.'

Do we not, therefore, need to take stock? Is there not much that passes for spirituality amongst us? The meetings are well-enough attended; there is plenty of activity; the speakers pass on their sermons; the assembly fund is well-enough looked after to support need in countries across the world and at home; the systems seem to work quite well but where is the reality of it all? God's people are often living semi-independent lives from one another and much of their lifestyle choices are no different to the world around them. Is it not time for us to examine what God is receiving and call out like the prophets of old, *'We have sinned'*? How many of us are mourning because of conditions in the land and longing for the simplicity of the presence of Christ?

Incidentally, it is mourners that are blessed not moaners. Looking back with rose-tinted spectacles does not help anyone. That spirit is to be rejected, it is not of God, it shrivels the saints and it lacks faith[26]. We need to look up. True mourners are entirely reliant on God and seek His glory. They are not preoccupied with the apparent faults of the saints or the supposed success of previous generations.

Having explained the difference between mourning and moaning, it might be wise, however, to briefly differentiate moaning from depression. Depression can be a very real medical condition that afflicts humans including God's people. We dare not belittle those who are going through the stress of mental ill health and should

[23]John 2.20: 'Then said the Jews, Forty and six years was this temple in building'.
[24]Daniel 9.5
[25]Nehemiah 1.6
[26]Ecclesiastes 7.10: 'Say not thou, What is the cause that the former days were better than these? for thou dost not enquire wisely concerning this.'

support them in any way that we can. Whilst we need to control negative thinking, we must acknowledge that all of us sometimes can experience thoughts coming upon us which are difficult to explain or eradicate. Whilst not the subject here, it is worth observing that positive thinking about Christ and our blessings and maintaining a life of good works for Christ can help our mental and spiritual health. Whilst the Lord referred to "*them that mourn in Zion*"[27] this does not mean that He wishes His people to be downcast or depressed. The Proverbs states: *'Commit thy works unto the LORD, and thy thoughts shall be established'*[28]. Notice it is committing 'our works' unto the Lord and not 'our thoughts' which is how we might have imagined the verse to read. In other words, keeping active in doing good works for the Lord is one of the best remedies for a positive mind set.

Our blessed Lord mourned because of conditions but never complained. He was *'sorrowful and very heavy'* and *'exceeding sorrowful'* in the Garden of Gethsemane[29]. Did He not wail over a city[30] and audibly cry for a people that He loved, lived for and ultimately would die for? Yet He never despaired, nor could He ever. Real tears[31] trickled down the Saviour's face at the harvest that sin had wrought at Bethany, but He was never morbid. He

[27]Isaiah 61.3

[28]Proverbs 16.3

[29]Matthew 26.37-38: 'And he took with him Peter and the two sons of Zebedee, and began to be sorrowful and very heavy. Then saith he unto them, My soul is exceeding sorrowful, even unto death: tarry ye here, and watch with me.'

[30]Luke 19.41-42: 'And when he was come near, he beheld the city, and wept over it, Saying, If thou hadst known, even thou, at least in this thy day, the things which belong unto thy peace! but now they are hid from thine eyes.'

[31]John 11.35: 'Jesus wept.'

'*rejoiced in spirit*'[32] and brought pleasure to His God and Father every moment of every day[33]. Although known as the '*Man of Sorrows*'[34] at God's right hand there is '*fulness of joy*'[35]. It is mourning in this spirit that the Lord has promised to bless. '*The joy of the Lord is your strength*'[36].

'For they shall'

His previous blessing had promised a present blessing to the humble – '*theirs is the kingdom of heaven*'- shocking the crowds who thought that the kingdom was only a future thought and could not be presently enjoyed. This second promise of Christ was also not a vague 'might be' nor a 'could be' but an emphatic '**shall be**'; this blessing to the mourner is a certainty. What an encouragement to all who are mourning because of conditions for God in our day – the Word of God says we shall be comforted[37].

'Be Comforted'

Comfort! This is exactly what we need. Comfort from the Triune God – from the Father of mercies, the *God of all comfort*[38]; the *comfort (consolation) in Christ*[39]; the *comfort of the Holy Spirit*[40] – flooding our souls with peace.

[32]Luke 10.21: 'In that hour Jesus rejoiced in spirit, and said, I thank thee, O Father, Lord of heaven and earth, that thou hast hid these things from the wise and prudent, and hast revealed them unto babes: even so, Father; for so it seemed good in thy sight.'

[33]John 8.29: 'And he that sent me is with me: the Father hath not left me alone; for I do always those things that please him.'

[34]Isaiah 53.3. 'He is despised and rejected of men; a man of sorrows, and acquainted with grief: and we hid as it were our faces from him; he was despised, and we esteemed him not.'

[35]Psalm 16.11: 'Thou wilt shew me the path of life: in thy presence is fulness of joy; at thy right hand there are pleasures for evermore.'

Through obedience to God's Word we derive the *'comfort of the Holy Scriptures'*[41] filling our minds with Christ[42] and alleviating our anxieties about doctrinal problems[43].

We also derive comfort from other believers. This is the one of the great purposes of Bible teaching to comfort each other[44]. The exploits of other believers can encourage us and so can their visits[45]. Furthermore, when God's people have been through trial, they are better equipped to comfort others when they too are going through trial and difficulty[46]. We need the comfort of one another to help us to continue in testimony for Him.

What a volume of truth is conveyed by the Lord's second beatitude: **'Blessed are they that mourn: for they shall be comforted.'**

[36]Nehemiah 8.10: 'Then he said unto them, Go your way, eat the fat, and drink the sweet, and send portions unto them for whom nothing is prepared: for this day is holy unto our Lord: neither be ye sorry; for the joy of the LORD is your strength.'

[37]Isaiah 61.3: 'To appoint unto them that mourn in Zion, to give unto them beauty for ashes, the oil of joy for mourning, the garment of praise for the spirit of heaviness; that they might be called trees of righteousness, the planting of the LORD, that he might be glorified.';

Jeremiah 31.13: 'Then shall the virgin rejoice in the dance, both young men and old together: for I will turn their mourning into joy, and will comfort them, and make them rejoice from their sorrow.'

[38]2 Corinthians 1.3: 'Blessed be God, even the Father of our Lord Jesus Christ, the Father of mercies, and the God of all comfort.'

[39]Philippians 2.1: 'If there be therefore any consolation in Christ, if any comfort of love, if any fellowship of the Spirit, if any bowels and mercies.'

[40]Acts 9.31: 'Then had the churches rest throughout all Judaea and Galilee and Samaria, and were edified; and walking in the fear of the Lord, and in the comfort of the Holy Ghost, were multiplied.'

[41]Romans 15.4: 'For whatsoever things were written aforetime were written for our learning, that we through patience and comfort of the scriptures might have hope.'

[42]Philippians 4.8-9: 'Finally, brethren, whatsoever things are true, whatsoever things are honest, whatsoever things are just, whatsoever things are pure, whatsoever things are lovely, whatsoever things are of good report; if there be any virtue, and if there be any praise, think on these things. Those things, which ye have both learned, and received, and heard, and seen in me, do: and the God of peace shall be with you.'

[43]1 Thessalonnians 4.18: 'Wherefore comfort one another with these words.'

[44]1 Corinthians 14.3: 'But he that prophesieth speaketh unto men to edification, and exhortation, and comfort.'

[45]2 Corinthians 7.6: 'Nevertheless God, that comforteth those that are cast down, comforted us by the coming of Titus.'

[46]2 Corinthians 1.4: 'Who comforteth us in all our tribulation, that we may be able to comfort them which are in any trouble, by the comfort wherewith we ourselves are comforted of God.'

Lesson

There will be great blessing for those that are deeply affected by the sin in this world and who will not accept superficial Christianity, believing that God deserves far better than this. What burdens me in this life? Am I aware of the great spiritual need all around me, and within? Or could it be I am taken up with my own self, and my mourning is more akin to self-pity?

Help, LORD; for the godly man ceaseth; for the faithful fail from among the children of men.

Psalm 12.1

Notes

Beatitude

Blessed Are The Meek:
For They Shall Inherit The Earth.

(Matthew 5.5)

The blessing of the self-restraining

'Blessed are the Meek'

The Lord had pronounced blessing and happiness to those who were humble in spirit and to those who were mourning due to the spiritual conditions of the land. Who would be included now in the third category of blessing?

The meek! The gathered throng would now realise that here was One who was different from all the other human leaders. They often emphasised in their rhetoric that those who wished to succeed should show strength (particularly of a military type), self-assertiveness even ruthlessness to achieve their goals. Modern philosophy has little changed this notion. The highest accolades are often given to those who are unbending and stubbornly un-diverted from their chosen course - particularly if the rewards are material or have increased entertainment value. The teaching of the Master was altogether different. Meekness was the source of happiness, not might.

The Saviour said of Himself that He was *'meek and lowly'*[47]. The prophet Zechariah had prophesied of Him riding into Jerusalem as the Messiah saying, *'Behold thy king cometh unto thee, meek'*[48]. The Saviour exhibited meekness but never encouraged or displayed weakness. Meekness is strength harnessed to the will of God, not spinelessness. Moses was (apart from our blessed Lord) the meekest man in all the earth[49] but he was not a weak character, far from it! The Lord Jesus acted in meekness when He allowed men to bind him with a cord of hemp. He who bound the might of the oceans with a strip of golden sand would allow Himself to be bound with a puny piece of string knotted by human hands[50]. In meekness He accepted the will of God that the creature of His own hand should crucify Him[51].

It was the Lord Jesus who ordered Peter to sheath his sword[52] and stooped down to pick Malchus' lacerated ear from the ground before restoring it perfectly to the side of his head in His last miracle before Calvary[53]. It was He who taught that the sheathed sword was more powerful than the drawn one[54]. Meekness is not the absence of might but the majesty of might.

---

[47]Matthew 11.29: 'Take my yoke upon you, and learn of me; for I am meek and lowly in heart: and ye shall find rest unto your souls.'

[48]Matthew 21.5: 'Tell ye the daughter of Sion, Behold, thy King cometh unto thee, meek, and sitting upon an ass, and a colt the foal of an ass.'

[49]Numbers 12.3: '(Now the man Moses was very meek, above all the men which were upon the face of the earth.)'

[50]Matthew 27.2: 'And when they had bound him, they led him away, and delivered him to Pontius Pilate the governor.'

[51]Matthew 20.18-19: 'Behold, we go up to Jerusalem; and the Son of man shall be betrayed unto the chief priests and unto the scribes, and they shall condemn him to death, And shall deliver him to the Gentiles to mock, and to scourge, and to crucify him: and the third day he shall rise again.'

The sword undrawn may tell of nobler merit
Than his who wars to win the laurel-crown
'Better', 'tis writ, 'to rule aright the spirit
Than take a town.'
Thy strength thy weakness is, if thou abuse it.
Thy courage cowardice, if uncontrolled.
To have the power to smite, and not to use it,
Is strength twofold.
(Bells and Pomegranates)

J. M. S. Tait

What about us? Our world is marked by selfishness, each one pursuing his goals. The career ladder is littered with people who have been trampled in the power-rush of colleagues. The Christian is to be different. We have higher orders to obey than the counsel of the world and a greater spiritual power within us to overcome the pressure of our base instincts. The fruit of the Spirit is to be kind, gracious and meek[55]. The meek person is prepared to sacrifice his own interests that those of others may be promoted. The woman who in meekness and in quiet dignity, honours and loves her husband, shunning the flaunting of wealth

[52]John 18.10-11: 'Then Simon Peter having a sword drew it, and smote the high priest's servant, and cut off his right ear. The servant's name was Malchus. Then said Jesus unto Peter, Put up thy sword into the sheath: the cup which my Father hath given me, shall I not drink it?'

[53]Luke 22.51: 'And Jesus answered and said, Suffer ye thus far. And he touched his ear, and healed him.'

[54]Matthew 26.52: 'Then said Jesus unto him, Put up again thy sword into his place: for all they that take the sword shall perish with the sword.' Luke 22.38: 'And they said, Lord, behold, here are two swords. And he said unto them, It is enough.'

[55]Galatians 5.22-23: 'But the fruit of the Spirit is love, joy, peace, longsuffering, gentleness, goodness, faith, meekness, temperance'.

and the materialistic lifestyle of the world, is of incalculable value to God[56]. It is the meek who are blessed, not the belligerent.

A true appreciation of this blessing would rid us from the pettiness, selfishness and rudeness that can afflict even the believer. The assembly is not a place for the assertion of our personal will, but strength harnessed to the will of God. It is the meekness of Christ that beautifies God's House.

'For they shall inherit the earth'

The earth! Are the blessings for the Church not all heavenly[57]? Perhaps the word "earth" here should be rendered, 'the land'. Israel did have hope of having a restored land, a physical inheritance, and this concept surely would be contained within such a blessing. The faithful would gain authority over cities in the coming Millennial Kingdom of Christ[58]! However, this blessing would also include the Church. Certainly, the Lord promised the apostles of the Church a tremendous blessing[59]. We too have a land that we are to enjoy inheriting now and in a day to come[60]. Our inheritance has a physical element to it as we reign over a Millennial earth in a coming day[61]. Furthermore, even Israel had a hope of 'the land' being an inheritance that was not physical[62];

[56] 1 Peter 3.3-4: 'Whose adorning let it not be that outward adorning of plaiting the hair, and of wearing of gold, or of putting on of apparel; But let it be the hidden man of the heart, in that which is not corruptible, even the ornament of a meek and quiet spirit, which is in the sight of God of great price.'

[57] Ephesians 1.3: 'Blessed be the God and Father of our Lord Jesus Christ, who hath blessed us with all spiritual blessings in heavenly places in Christ.'

[58] Luke 19.17: 'And he said unto him, Well, thou good servant: because thou hast been faithful in a very little, have thou authority over ten cities.'

a land greater than the soil and stone of earth, even one which was eternal and God-given. The Saviour is promising that those who exhibit a meekness of spirit will not only know blessing and happiness in the present but will enjoy the spiritual inheritance of the "land" both now and eternally. That is something worth investing in! Let us go in for displaying meekness and be blessed of God.

[59]Matthew 19.28-29: 'And Jesus said unto them, Verily I say unto you, That ye which have followed me, in the regeneration when the Son of man shall sit in the throne of his glory, ye also shall sit upon twelve thrones, judging the twelve tribes of Israel. And every one that hath forsaken houses, or brethren, or sisters, or father, or mother, or wife, or children, or lands, for my name's sake, shall receive an hundredfold, and shall inherit everlasting life.'

[60]Hebrews 12.22: 'But ye are come unto mount Sion, and unto the city of the living God, the heavenly Jerusalem, and to an innumerable company of angels';

Hebrews 13.14: 'For here have we no continuing city, but we seek one to come.'

[61]Revelation 3.21: 'To him that overcometh will I grant to sit with me in my throne, even as I also overcame, and am set down with my Father in his throne.';

1 Cor. 6.2: 'Do ye not know that the saints shall judge the world?'

[62]Hebrews 11.16: 'But now they desire a better country, that is, an heavenly: wherefore God is not ashamed to be called their God: for he hath prepared for them a city.'

Lesson

There will be great rewards for those whose lives are governed and bound by the will of God and not self-will. To what extent am I marked by "a meek and quiet spirit"?

The meek shall eat and be satisfied: they shall praise the LORD that seek him: your heart shall live for ever.

Psalm 22.26

Notes

$\mathscr{B}$eatitude

Blessed Are They Which Do Hunger and Thirst After
Righteousness: For They Shall Be Filled.

(Matthew 5.6)

The blessing for those who are striving and hungering for righteousness

$\mathscr{T}$he fourth category of people who are to be blessed are those who have a ravenous desire for God's righteousness; people whose pursuits are entirely spiritual, the bent of whose life is heavenly.

'Blessed are they which do hunger and thirst after righteousness'

This "righteousness" of course could be limited to mean those people who desire to be reckoned righteous before God. Being reckoned or constituted righteous is a wonderful truth and is enjoyed by all believers through faith in the Lord Jesus Christ: *'being justified (declared righteous) by faith, we have peace with God through our Lord Jesus Christ'*[63]. Salvation provides a legal basis in God's sight for constituting us righteous through simply repenting of our sin and believing on the Lord Jesus for salvation[64]. The

---

[63]Romans 5.1

[64]Romans 3.22: 'Even the righteousness of God which is by faith of Jesus Christ unto all and upon all them that believe.'

'imputed' or 'constituted' righteousness that Abraham was granted can also now be enjoyed by us on the same basis – faith alone[65]. Both Abraham at the outset of the Bible, along with believers today, enjoy this 'righteousness' because of the same fact: Christ's death and resurrection have provided a righteous basis for God to forgive sins and impute righteousness[66] in the past and now in the present.

However, this fourth blessing appears to contain a wider thought than even the glorious truth of being regarded as righteous before God. The fulfilment of this "blessing" is to those whose appetite can only be satisfied by feeding on the righteousness of God; those whose ambition is to be consumed with the will of God. If this is the case it certainly narrows the field of those who can enjoy this beatitude!

The metaphor of hunger and thirst can be appreciated to varying degrees by everyone at a human level. The need for food and drink to sustain human life is a self-evident truth to all. Our blessed Lord transfers this thought to people craving for God Himself with all their body, soul and spirit. Christ alone is the One who satisfies their longings. The Lord Jesus said of Himself, *'I am the bread of Life'*.

[65]Romans 4.22-25: 'And therefore it was imputed to him [Abraham] for righteousness. Now it was not written for his sake alone, that it was imputed to him; But for us also, to whom it shall be imputed, if we believe on him that raised up Jesus our Lord from the dead; Who was delivered for our offences, and was raised again for our justification.'
[66]Romans 3.25-26: 'Whom God hath set forth to be a propitiation through faith in his blood, to declare his righteousness for the remission of sins that are past, through the forbearance of God; To declare, I say, at this time his righteousness: that he might be just, and the justifier of him which believeth in Jesus'.

Not many have reached this high ground. The Psalmist did: *'as the hart (deer) pants after the water brook so pants my soul after thee O God'*[67]; *'I opened my mouth and panted: for I longed for thy commandments'*[68]; *'with my whole heart have I sought thee'*[69]. Paul also had this craving for God exclaiming: *'That I may know him'*[70].

Perhaps we all must confess that we have rarely laid claim to this ground. Maybe over a serious bereavement of a loved one, or during a deep personal issue, our soul was lost in God. On the occasion when we are around the bread and wine on a Lord's Day are our souls not lost in wonder at Christ and our hearts bubbling up in worship? It certainly should be the case[71].

Are these experiences irregular because our lives have become so worldly? This does not necessarily mean sinful but certainly full of activity which is not spiritual. One thousand priorities come into our lives and what part of our lives does God get? Malachi asked a solemn question: *'Will a man rob God?'*[72] The answer that is given is, "Yes, we can!". In an absolute sense, of course, we can add nothing to God and take nothing from Him because God is entirely self-sufficient[73]. However, God demands from us our whole life[74] and we can rob God of many things - for example, our time, talents, mind, and worship.

[67]Psalm 42.1
[68]Psalm 119.131
[69]Psalm 119.10
[70]Philippians 3.10
[71]Psalm 45.1: 'My heart is inditing (bubbling up) a good matter: I speak of the things which I have made touching the king: my tongue is the pen of a ready writer.'
[72]Malachi 3.8
[73]Acts 17.25: 'Neither is worshipped with men's hands, as though he needed any thing, seeing he giveth to all life, and breath, and all things.'

Our blessed Lord always craved the will of His God and Father. His meat and drink were to do the will of Him that sent Him[75]. His every moment, motive, and movement was entirely in harmony with the will of the Father. His zeal for His Father's House consumed Him[76]. He longed for righteousness to be the desired portion of His people. He prayed, indeed wailed, for a city that refused Him[77].

How are we doing? Are we playing at spiritual things? Is not the great weakness amongst us that the world has come into our thinking, lives, homes, and assemblies, squeezing out desires for God's Word?

Have our taste buds been whetted for worldly entertainment and the desires after the will of God become an uncommon experience. If this is so, let us repent and feel the eternal force of His words: *"Blessed are they which do hunger and thirst after righteousness"*.

'For they shall be filled'

The promise to those whose life conforms to the will of God is that they shall be filled. Deep spiritual satisfaction is assured only to such. There is a contentment that is even beyond godliness, for *'godliness with contentment is great gain'*[78]. That desire for a deeper

---

[74]Romans 12.1-2: 'I beseech you therefore, brethren, by the mercies of God, that ye present your bodies a living sacrifice, holy, acceptable unto God, which is your reasonable service. And be not conformed to this world: but be ye transformed by the renewing of your mind, that ye may prove what is that good, and acceptable, and perfect, will of God.'

[75]John 4.34: 'Jesus saith unto them, My meat is to do the will of him that sent me, and to finish his work.'

[76]John 2.17: 'And his disciples remembered that it was written, The zeal of thine house hath eaten me up.'

knowledge of God and of His righteousness is the cry of all true believers[79]. A craving for His Word and an inner motivation to do His will leads ultimately to inner tranquillity and peace. Paul describes it as being *'filled with all the fulness of God'* [80]. The word *'filled'* is often used in the physical sense of being full of food[81] but here it is being used in a spiritual sense. The same word is used of Lazarus craving crumbs from the rich man's table[82]. The Lord spoke of Himself as being the 'Bread of Life' elevating food to beyond the physical level[83]. He promised that those who received Him would *'never hunger'*. The promise in this beatitude goes even further than 'not ever hungering'. The Lord Jesus is promising believers complete spiritual satisfaction if they are hungry for righteousness. What a promise!

This contentment can be enjoyed despite adverse personal and physical circumstances. Paul said he had been taught this amazing truth: *'I have learned, in whatsoever state I am, therewith to be content'*[84]. The Hebrew writer exhorts: *'Be content with such things as ye have: for he hath said, I will never leave thee, nor forsake thee'*[85].

The cares of this life can press upon us and making ends meet can be really challenging for believers, even in the Western world. However, we need to learn the lessons of Christ that *'our Father knoweth that we have need of these things'*, and we can cast our care upon Him. Let us go in for hungering and thirsting after righteousness and we shall be filled.

[77]Luke 19.41-44: 'And when he was come near, he beheld the city, and wept over it, Saying, If thou hadst known, even thou, at least in this thy day, the things which belong unto thy peace! but now they are hid from thine eyes. For the days shall come upon thee, that thine enemies shall cast a trench about thee, and compass thee round, and keep thee in on

every side, And shall lay thee even with the ground, and thy children within thee; and they shall not leave in thee one stone upon another; because thou knewest not the time of thy visitation.'

[78]1 Timothy 6.6

[79]Philippians 3.10-12: 'That I may know him, and the power of his resurrection, and the fellowship of his sufferings, being made conformable unto his death; If by any means I might attain unto the resurrection of the dead. Not as though I had already attained, either were already perfect: but I follow after, if that I may apprehend that for which also I am apprehended of Christ Jesus.'

[80]Ephesians 3.19

[81]Matthew 14.20; 15.33, 37

[82]Luke 16.21: 'And desiring to be fed with the crumbs which fell from the rich man's table: moreover the dogs came and licked his sores.'

[83]John 6.35: 'And Jesus said unto them, I am the bread of life: he that cometh to me shall never hunger; and he that believeth on me shall never thirst.'

[84]Philippians 4.11

[85]Hebrews 13.5

Lesson

We shall be fully satisfied and filled when we desire, follow and feed on Christ and His righteousness. What do I crave in this life? What is taking up my thoughts and energies at this point in my life?

I have esteemed the words of his mouth more than my necessary food.

Job 23.12

Notes

eatitude

Blessed Are The Merciful: For They Shall
Obtain Mercy.

(Matthew 5.7)

The blessing to the sympathetic and those sensitive to others

$\mathscr{B}$ lessed are the merciful! This was a different strain of teaching to what the people were used to hearing. They had to listen to the meticulous, legalistic interpretation of the law laboriously laid out by the religious leaders. Hearing the Saviour say, 'Blessed are the compassionate' would sound so different and so touching. It is the opposite to vengeance or vindictiveness or the insistence of retribution or retaliation. He declared that the "happy" were those who adopted a merciful, forgiving attitude, a new concept to the Pharisee.

God's mercy is often defined as the restraining of God's wrath to those who deserve it. As believers, for example, we deserved eternal death and it was only through God's mercy we could be saved: *'Not by works of righteousness which we have done, but according to his mercy he saved us'*[86].

Mercy, however, also carries the thought of pity and deep compassion which fits the context here. For another example of

---

[86]Titus 3. 5

this meaning of mercy, consider the experiences of Epaphroditus and Paul in the Philippian epistle: *'For indeed he was sick nigh unto death: but God had mercy on him; and not on him only, but on me also, lest I should have sorrow upon sorrow'*[87].

It is fascinating that Matthew's Gospel, which was written primarily to the Jew, is full of mercy towards the Gentiles. In chapter 2 men from the East[88], those outside of the commonwealth of Israel, are the first documented in Matthew as seeing the Christ. The people that sat in darkness who saw the great light in chapter 4 were in Galilee of the Gentiles.[89] In chapter 8, a Roman centurion had more faith than anyone else in Israel[90] and in chapter 15 mercy is shown to a Syrophoenician woman[91] – someone from outside the boundaries of Israel. The mercy of God is available to all in the world who repent of their sins. This is a theme throughout Matthew which is why it ends with the judgment of the living nations[92] and the great commission: *'Go ye therefore, and teach all nations'*[93].

God has shown great mercy to us and He expects to see this exhibited in our lives. In chapter 6, this theme of forgiveness

[87]Philippians 2. 27

[88]Matthew 2. 1-2: 'Now when Jesus was born in Bethlehem of Judaea in the days of Herod the king, behold, there came wise men from the east to Jerusalem, Saying, Where is he that is born King of the Jews? for we have seen his star in the east, and are come to worship him'.

[89]Matthew 4. 15-16: 'The land of Zabulon, and the land of Nephthalim, by the way of the sea, beyond Jordan, Galilee of the Gentiles; The people which sat in darkness saw great light; and to them which sat in the region and shadow of death light is sprung up'.

[90]Matthew 8. 10: 'When Jesus heard it, he marvelled, and said to them that followed, Verily I say unto you, I have not found so great faith, no, not in Israel.'

[91]Matthew 15. 21-22: 'Then Jesus went thence, and departed into the

is taken up by the Lord as He exhorts His own, who have experienced mercy, to forgive others: *'forgive us our debts, as we forgive our debtors.... if ye forgive not men their trespasses, neither will your Father forgive...'*[94]. He reminds them that unforgiving behaviour will boomerang back on us: *'For with what judgment ye judge, ye shall be judged: and with what measure ye mete, it shall be measured to you again'*[95].

In chapter 9, the Lord Jesus forgives the sins of the palsied man, showing that mercy and forgiveness were more important than the ability to be active and walk[96], but in verse 13 in the same chapter He states that mercy is more important than sacrifice: *'I will have mercy, and not sacrifice'*[97]. Later in chapter 12, he condemned the Jews for not adhering to this injunction: *'But if ye had known what this meaneth, I will have mercy, and not sacrifice'*[98]. He authoritatively condemned their neglect of mercy: *"Woe unto you, scribes and Pharisees, hypocrites! for ye pay tithe of mint and anise and cummin, and have omitted the weightier matters of the law, judgment, mercy and faith"*[99]. Are we guilty of a lack of compassion and forgiveness as we seek to uphold the truth?

coasts of Tyre and Sidon. And, behold, a woman of Canaan came out of the same coasts, and cried unto him, saying, Have mercy on me, O Lord, thou Son of David.'

[92]Matthew 25. 31-32: 'When the Son of man shall come in his glory, and all the holy angels with him, then shall he sit upon the throne of his glory: And before him shall be gathered all nations: and he shall separate them one from another, as a shepherd divideth his sheep from the goats.'

[93]Matthew 28. 19: 'Go ye therefore, and teach all nations, baptizing them in the name of the Father, and of the Son, and of the Holy Ghost.'

[94]Matthew 6. 12-15

[95]Matthew 7. 2. Compare also James 2. 13: 'For he shall have judgment without mercy, that hath shewed no mercy; and mercy rejoiceth against judgment.'

In chapter 18, as He introduces the wonderful subject of the local assembly He does so in the context of forgiveness and mercy. Indeed, after He has introduced the subject Peter asks: *'Lord, how oft shall my brother sin against me, and I forgive him? till seven times?'*[100]. We all know the extraordinary reply of the Saviour as He tells him to multiply that another seventy times[101]! He follows this teaching with the parable on mercy and forgiveness where the Master in the parable says: *"Shouldest not thou also have had compassion on thy fellow servant, even as I had pity on thee?*[102]. How solemn!

Matthew is the gospel of compassion where acts of mercy such as giving a drink of cold water to a righteous man will be rewarded[103]. The Saviour is heard to say to His own, *'Come, ye blessed of my Father... for I was an hungred, and ye gave me meat: I was thirsty, and ye gave me drink: I was a stranger, and ye took me in: Naked, and ye clothed me: I was sick, and ye visited me: I was in prison, and ye came unto me.'*[104]. Do these features mark us?

This beatitude is so searching. How many issues in the lives of believers are due to a lack of mercy and a lack of compassion?

[96]Matthew 9. 2-5: 'And, behold, they brought to him a man sick of the palsy, lying on a bed: and Jesus seeing their faith said unto the sick of the palsy; Son, be of good cheer; thy sins be forgiven thee. And, behold, certain of the scribes said within themselves, This man blasphemeth. And Jesus knowing their thoughts said, Wherefore think ye evil in your hearts? For whether is easier, to say, Thy sins be forgiven thee; or to say, Arise, and walk?'.
[97]Matthew 9. 13
[98]Matthew 12. 7
[99]Matthew 23. 23
[100]Matthew 18. 21

The Lord is teaching that mercy is essential as a disciple and is a prerequisite to happiness. Harbouring feelings of indignation or spite or anger against our brother and sister will lead to great grief. Acts of kindness and mercy will be eternally blessed. This is the reason why so much of the Lord's ministry was focused on this subject and why it is so pointed. **Blessed are the merciful** is a timeless principle which should be the guiding motto for every believer.

'For they shall obtain mercy'

In return we will know the pity and compassion of the Lord. We have already been forgiven and so we should be able to forgive others:

'Be ye kind one to another, tenderhearted, forgiving one another, even as God for Christ's sake hath forgiven you.'[105]

He cares for us. He understands us even when no one else does. We have a great High Priest who is passed through the heavens, Jesus the Son of God, who is affected by our circumstances and who Himself is able to sympathise as One who has passed this way before us. He has made it possible for us to approach a throne of grace in order to obtain 'mercy' – pity and compassion - and help in our hour of need[106]. What a blessing!

[101]Matthew 18. 22: 'Jesus saith unto him, I say not unto thee, Until seven times: but, Until seventy times seven.'
[102]Matthew 18. 33
[103]Matthew 10. 42: 'And whosoever shall give to drink unto one of these little ones a cup of cold water only in the name of a disciple, verily I say unto you, he shall in no wise lose his reward.'

[104]Matthew 25. 34-40

[105]Ephesians 4. 32

[106]Hebrews 4. 14-16: 'Seeing then that we have a great high priest, that is passed into the heavens, Jesus the Son of God, let us hold fast our profession. For we have not an high priest which cannot be touched with the feeling of our infirmities; but was in all points tempted like as we are, yet without sin. Let us therefore come boldly unto the throne of grace, that we may obtain mercy, and find grace to help in time of need.'

Lesson

Showing love and compassion to others should be a feature of all followers of Christ and will be recompensed. In blessing others, God will bless us. To what extent am I known for my compassion and authentic concern for others?

The LORD is gracious, and full of compassion; slow to anger, and of great mercy.

Psalm 145.8

Notes

eatitude

Blessed Are The Pure In Heart: For They Shall
See God.

(Matthew 5.8)

The blessing of the sanctified

*T*he Saviour never looked for applause from men. His message was not designed to court popularity – *'blessed are the pure in heart'.* Men love to parade external holiness – especially in religious ceremony through wearing so called "holy" vestments and participating in public acts of "sanctified" service - but inner purity of the heart is rare. Indeed, the only man who lived fully in the good of this beatitude was the Lord Jesus Himself. His outward acts and inner motives and thoughts were always pure and holy, even under the direct attack of the Devil[107]. *"In Him is no sin[108], He knew no sin[109] and He did no sin"[110].* One of the reasons why the inner parts of the Burnt Offering were washed in water[111] was because it had to be a fitting type of our blessed Lord who was inwardly pure and unable to sin[112]. He was the God who *"desired truth in the inward parts"[113].*

---

[107]John 14. 30: 'Hereafter I will not talk much with you: for the prince of this world cometh, and hath nothing in me.'

[108]1 John 3. 5

[109]2 Corinthians 5. 21

[110]1 Peter 2. 22

[111]Leviticus 1. 9: 'But his inwards and his legs shall he wash in water: and the priest shall burn all on the altar, to be a burnt sacrifice, an offering made by fire, of a sweet savour unto the LORD.'

But this beatitude is intended to be kept by us. Our blessed Lord expects us to be inwardly clean (the word 'pure' is unique in the English translation of the gospels but it is normally translated 'clean'). He will shortly warn that looking on a woman with lust is "adultery" in the heart[114]. This age-old sin has stained every generation. In our generation, however, the issue has been extended as modern technology has made readily available filthy images onto mobile phones and computers. What was once done in the dark is now brazenly beamed into the minds of children as well as adults. Let us take steps to guard our minds and be careful what we allow in our lives and homes. Christian parents need to be exercised about what their children can access. Some software controls, for example, can save our children from severe problems. The devil wants to destroy them. Purity is not a preference but the primary purpose of Christianity. The Lord asked us to pluck out our eye if it was a problem[115]. He was not speaking literally, of course, but the strength of language indicates the severity of the divine displeasure of uncleanness of heart and the extent to which we must go to remain pure! We **cannot** sup at the Lord's table and the table of demons[116]. He will not tolerate this.

But purity of the heart would also include our motives – the Lord also spoke of the "mixed" eye[117]. This exhortation comes after He

[112]Hebrews 4. 15: 'For we have not a high priest not able to sympathise with our infirmities, but tempted in all things in like manner, sin apart.' (Darby);

James 1. 13: 'Let no man say when he is tempted, I am tempted of God: for God cannot be tempted with evil, neither tempteth he any man.'
[113]Psalm 51.6
[114]Matthew 5.28
[115]Matthew 5.29: 'And if thy right eye offend thee, pluck it out, and cast it from thee: for it is profitable for thee that one of thy members should perish, and not that thy whole body should be cast into hell.'

had warned about *laying not up treasure in earth* and *'where your treasure is, there will your heart be also'*[118]. If deep down in my heart I am motivated by material things and financial reward, my life will be full of darkness, and He added solemnly, *'how great is that darkness'*. Perhaps the greatest hindrance to spiritual blessing is material pursuits and desires. God's people are stifled by the world. We should be thoughtful about what our hearts are dwelling upon and treasuring. Guard your heart, for everything else flows from it.

It is in Matthew's gospel, more than all the others, that the whole issue of the heart is developed. It is in Matthew, for example, that the depths of evil in the human heart are fully described[119]. There were those drawing near to Him but *'their heart (was) far from him,'*[120] and even a servant who claims to be waiting for his lord "*in his heart*" says *'My lord delayeth his coming'*[121]. The Lord called him an *evil servant*. It is in Matthew that the *'lowly in heart'*[122] are blessed and disciples are encouraged to love the Lord "*with all their heart'*[123]. Let us, therefore, *'keep [our] heart with all diligence; for out of it are the issues of life'*[124].

The Lord is emphasising at the outset of His public teaching the important principle of righteousness in His kingdom.

[116]1 Corinthians 10. 21

[117]Matthew 6.22-23: 'The light of the body is the eye: if therefore thine eye be single, thy whole body shall be full of light. But if thine eye be evil, thy whole body shall be full of darkness. If therefore the light that is in thee be darkness, how great is that darkness!'

[118]Matthew 6. 21

[119]Matthew 15.18-19: 'But those things which proceed out of the mouth come forth from the heart; and they defile the man. For out of the heart proceed evil thoughts, murders, adulteries, fornications, thefts, false witness, blasphemies:'

Righteousness is also a theme in Matthew – more than all the other gospels combined. It is here that the first recorded words of Christ are: *'thus it becometh us to fulfil all righteousness'*[125]. In this gospel we are told that there will be a reward for those who receive a *'righteous man'*[126] and it describes a future day when the *'righteous shall shine forth as the sun in the kingdom'*[127]. There is much that masquerades as Christianity and is manifestly unrighteous. Christians, be on your guard – God's kingdom is righteous.

'They shall see God'

This is a unique expression in the gospels. There is a sense in which *'no man hath seen God at any time'*[128]. However, the "Son" has fully revealed Him. We see the Father in the person of the Son. He said, *'He that hath seen me hath seen the Father'*[129]. The promise to those who have clean hands and a pure heart is that they can ascend into the hill of the Lord[130]; they can see something of the glory of God. The Hebrew writer says: *'Follow ... holiness, without which no man shall see the Lord'*[131].

Of course, this blessed promise will come true to all believers. David could say: *'As for me, I shall behold thy face in righteousness:*

[120]Matthew 15. 8

[121]Matthew 24. 48

[122]Matthew 11. 29

[123]Matthew 22.37: 'Jesus said unto him, Thou shalt love the Lord thy God with all thy heart, and with all thy soul, and with all thy mind.'

[124]Proverbs 4.23

[125]Matthew 3.15: 'And Jesus answering said unto him, Suffer it to be so now: for thus it becometh us to fulfil all righteousness. Then he suffered him.'

[126]Matthew 10.41: 'He that receiveth a prophet in the name of a prophet shall receive a prophet's reward; and he that receiveth a righteous man in the name of a righteous man shall receive a righteous man's reward.'

I shall be satisfied, when I awake, with thy likeness'[132]. **Then shall** *'his servants serve him: and they shall see his face; and his name shall be in their foreheads'*[133]. **They** *'shall see him as he is'*[134].

What a blessing there is for those who go in for purity of heart – they shall see God.

[127]Matthew 13.43: 'Then shall the righteous shine forth as the sun in the kingdom of their Father. Who hath ears to hear, let him hear.'

[128]John 1. 18: 'No man hath seen God at any time; the only begotten Son, which is in the bosom of the Father, he hath declared him.'

[129]John 14.9: 'Jesus saith unto him, Have I been so long time with you, and yet hast thou not known me, Philip? he that hath seen me hath seen the Father; and how sayest thou then, Shew us the Father?'

[130]Psalm 24. 3-4: 'Who shall ascend into the hill of the LORD? or who shall stand in his holy place? He that hath clean hands, and a pure heart; who hath not lifted up his soul unto vanity, nor sworn deceitfully.'

[131]Hebrews 12. 14: 'Follow peace with all men, and holiness, without which no man shall see the Lord.'

John 16.22: 'And ye now therefore have sorrow: but I will see you again, and your heart shall rejoice, and your joy no man taketh from you.'

[132]Psalm 17.15

[133]Revelation 22. 3-4: 'And there shall be no more curse: but the throne of God and of the Lamb shall be in it; and his servants shall serve him: And they shall see his face; and his name shall be in their foreheads.'

[134]1 John 3. 2: 'Beloved, now are we the sons of God, and it doth not yet appear what we shall be: but we know that, when he shall appear, we shall be like him; for we shall see him as he is.'

Lesson

Holiness of heart is a prerequisite to the revelation of God's glory. Our lives must be guided by the lamp of God's Word, and our eyes and minds filled with His light. There should be no "dark corners" in a Christian's life.

With the pure thou wilt shew thyself pure; and with the froward (devious) thou wilt shew thyself froward.

Psalm 18.26

Notes

Beatitude

Blessed Are The Peacemakers:
For They Shall Be Called the Children of God.

(Matthew 5.9)

The blessing of sonship

*T*he Lord's view of the world was diametrically different from the political, religious and military leaders that were alive then, and those that are in power generally today. The Psalmist could lament in his day: *'I am for peace: but when I speak, they are for war'*[135]. There is much that masquerades as peace today but really it is high-powered negotiations over power, wealth, resources, territory, position, with the threat of military action if the negotiations are unsuccessful. The soft silk glove of diplomacy lies firmly upon the hard, clenched fist of power. The world continues to war and fight. There are more wars today than at any time in human history. One day the King of Peace will arise and reign on this earth and peace will flow *like a river*[136] and *'nation shall not lift up a sword against nation neither shall they learn war any more'*[137].

---

[135]Psalm 120.7

[136]Isaiah 66.12: 'For thus saith the LORD, Behold, I will extend peace to her like a river, and the glory of the Gentiles like a flowing stream: then shall ye suck, ye shall be borne upon her sides, and be dandled upon her knees.'

[137]Micah 4.3

Leaving aside politics and human government, what is our position in relation to peace-making?

- Do we ever scheme about others or speak behind their back?
- Do we encourage rivalry or divisive behaviour?
- Do we exploit weakness in others for our advantage?

As believers, this behaviour should be abhorrent to us. It is the antithesis of Christianity. The first stirrings of this fleshly attitude in our hearts should be dealt with severely and we must pray for grace to *'live peaceably with all'*[138]. We must stand aside and be different when we see this type of behaviour in the office, school, college or, tragically, the assembly of believers. This is where the world can see Christianity in action more than anywhere else. Christians should be transparent, friendly, honest, impartial and true. This is a real testimony to Christ.

Divisive behaviour certainly has no place amongst us as believers in assembly fellowship. Of course, problems can arise between believers. Shortly after He uttered this wonderful beatitude our Lord Jesus gave ministry on reconciliation. He made it clear that we should *'first be reconciled'* to our brother[139] before we should try to worship before God. In other words, we must have good relations with the saints before our lives can be pleasing to God. The Lord had already raised subject of forgiveness in the fifth beatitude – *'blessed are the merciful'*. We have already seen that forgiveness is a theme in Matthew's Gospel. The word 'peacemaker' is also unique to Matthew. It is no surprise, therefore, that the subject

[138]Romans 12.18: 'If it be possible, as much as lieth in you, live peaceably with all men.'

[139]Matthew 5.24: 'Leave there thy gift before the altar, and go thy way; first be reconciled to thy brother, and then come and offer thy gift.'

of restoration and reconciliation is never far from the Saviour's ministry in Matthew[140]. It anticipates a day when all things shall be restored, and the Messiah will reign in peace. Of course, He is the unique peacemaker for He *made peace through the blood of his cross*[141]. His offer of peace to the world is, therefore, based on sacrifice and not compromise. We are the beneficiaries of His peace; *He is our Peace* said Paul to the Ephesians[142]. He has removed the *enmity* between God and Man in His death and has laid a basis for reconciling *all things unto himself*. One day this world will know peace all because of Him. As believers, we are currently in the position of being *reconciled to God*[143] and now have *peace with God*[144] and can presently enjoy His *peace which passes all understanding*[145].

However, this blessing leaves believers with a big responsibility. He has left us to be peacemakers now in this world. Peacemakers are those who strive to prevent contention, strife and war; they use their influence to reconcile opposing parties, and to prevent hostilities in families, neighbourhoods and assemblies. Everyone

[140]Matthew 5.24 (see above); Matthew 17. 11: 'And Jesus answered and said unto them, Elias truly shall first come, and restore all things.'

[141]Colossians 1.20-21: 'And, having made peace through the blood of his cross, by him to reconcile all things unto himself; by him, I say, whether they be things in earth, or things in heaven. And you, that were sometime alienated and enemies in your mind by wicked works, yet now hath he reconciled'.

[142]Ephesians 2.14-15: 'For he is our peace, who hath made both one, and hath broken down the middle wall of partition between us; Having abolished in his flesh the enmity, even the law of commandments contained in ordinances; for to make in himself of twain one new man, so making peace'.

[143]2 Corinthians 5.20-21: 'Now then we are ambassadors for Christ, as though God did beseech you by us: we pray you in Christ's stead, be ye

may do something of this; and no-one is more like God than he/she who does it. This does not mean we can officiously and insensitively interfere in anything that is none of our business; but we can do much to promote peace. There are those who can bring together opposing parties. These matters are better to be dealt with quickly before positions become entrenched. Long and deadly quarrels might often be prevented by early reconciliation. The peacemaker will be tender hearted in spirit. Paul says, *'be ye kind one to another, tenderhearted, forgiving one another, even as God for Christ's sake hath forgiven you'*[146]. Sadly, the reverse can be true, and the saints can be extremely hurtful to one another[147]: *'these things ought not so to be'*[148].

'Shall be called the children (sons) of God'

Peacemakers are called sons - those who resemble God, the author of peace[149]. The theme of sonship appears more in Matthew than any other gospel. Sonship is different to childhood. A child speaks of birth, lineage, genealogy perhaps even immaturity. Sonship speaks of dignity and character reflecting the glory and honour of the Father. All believers are called to be sons[150]. Those who manifest a spirit of promoting peace are like God and are therefore worthy to be called sons of God. May God help us to be peacemakers and be worthy of being called His sons.

reconciled to God. For he hath made him to be sin for us, who knew no sin; that we might be made the righteousness of God in him.'

[144]Romans 5.1: 'Therefore being justified by faith, we have peace with God through our Lord Jesus Christ'.

[145]Philippians 4.7: 'And the peace of God, which passeth all understanding, shall keep your hearts and minds through Christ Jesus'.

[146]Ephesians 4.32

[147]Galatians 5.15: 'But if ye bite and devour one another, take heed that ye be not consumed one of another.'

[148]James 3.10

[149]1 Corinthians 14.33: 'For God is not the author of confusion, but of peace, as in all churches of the saints.'

[150]Galatians 3.26: 'For ye are all the children (sons) of God by faith in Christ Jesus.'

1 John 3.1-2: 'Behold, what manner of love the Father hath bestowed upon us, that we should be called the sons of God: therefore the world knoweth us not, because it knew him not. Beloved, now are we the sons of God, and it doth not yet appear what we shall be: but we know that, when he shall appear, we shall be like him; for we shall see him as he is'.

Lesson

"If possible, as much as lieth in **you** *live peaceably with all men"* (Romans 12.18). Seek to bring peace to others and make peace between those who are opposing one another. In so doing you will be a true son of God and will live a life pleasing to the Father. We should never be offensive to others, but equally we should be slow to take offence ourselves. To what extent am I easy to get along with in the local assembly of which I am part; at my work; in my home; with my neighbours?

Seek peace and pursue it.

Psalm 34.14

Her ways are ways of pleasantness, and all her paths are peace.

Proverbs 3.17

And be ye kind one to another, tenderhearted, forgiving one another, even as God for Christ's sake hath forgiven you.

Ephesians 4.32

Notes

Blessed Are They Which Are Persecuted For Righteousness'
Sake: For Theirs Is The Kingdom Of Heaven.

(Matthew 5.10)

The blessing to the suffering

$\mathscr{T}$he Lord's promise of persecution for His followers would not be the usual way a leader tries to recruit, but we have already seen how His teaching was altogether different from that of men. The Lord Jesus was always honest and becoming a Christian was and still is a difficult path, a "narrow way". He promised His followers **persecution** and then told them that they were blessed.

Blessed? Persecution had been something to abhor, shirk or run from, but not embrace as a blessing. The Jewish people had had their fill of Roman oppression; their history was full of marauding forces that had raped the land and destroyed the nation. Why would they consider persecution a blessing?

They would listen again to the Lord saying that the blessing would be to those who were persecuted for righteousness' sake. This would cause them to stop and consider. This persecution was not for a political cause, for national territory, economic advantage or the advancement of a religious ideology, but for personal righteousness. This was altogether different. No teacher had ever said anything remotely like this. Other kingdoms had been built on the principles of war and oppression. He said that the kingdom of heaven was built on the highest and noblest of principles - righteousness.

A kingdom built on this principle would not be popular. It was much easier to be persecuted for what you did, or what you believed in, than for your holy character and righteous life. His followers would subsequently learn that to be associated with Him had high demands and would result in them being despised, ridiculed and treated with contempt; in some cases, it would mean a violent and premature death. Our Lord warned His own of this, saying, *'they will also persecute you'*[151]. Paul claimed that, *'all that will live godly in Christ Jesus shall suffer persecution'*[152]. This was not scaremongering; many of Christ's followers have suffered immense persecution down through the ages.

He, of course, was persecuted for righteousness' sake. In one sense He was the only One to be truly persecuted for righteousness, as all others have aspects of their conduct which is unrighteous. Paul records, *'there is none righteous, no, not one'*[153]. However, they could not find one error in Christ, not one word that needed to be revoked, not one slip, not even a mistimed action or word or a mistaken action. Indeed, even His motives were transparent and righteous. And yet, *'they crucified him*[154]*'*. They tried to attribute His power to the devil, they cast aspersions on His virgin birth, they

---

[151]John 15. 20-21: 'Remember the word that I said unto you, The servant is not greater than his lord. If they have persecuted me, they will also persecute you; if they have kept my saying, they will keep yours also. But all these things will they do unto you for my name's sake, because they know not him that sent me.'
[152]2 Timothy 3.12
[153]Romans 3. 10

claimed He was mad, and, ultimately, they crucified Him for His claim that He was the Son of God[155]. The Man who made the blind to see was blindfolded and struck with a rod on the face; the Man who took the five loaves into His hands and broke the bread and fed the multitudes had crude nails hammered through them. His righteous life brought out their contempt and envy that Pilate fully understood[156] yet failed to condemn.

The Lord, therefore, warned that those who followed in this path of righteousness would face persecution. Christianity is not popular. Young Christians will soon find that their actions will draw out contempt and ridicule or worse: "This is the way the Master went, should not the servant tread it still?[157]" Take heart, this is the way of blessing, the Saviour said. Not only will you be blessed, but you will bless others. This world is full of unrighteousness and a simple believer walking in the *paths of righteousness*[158] will bring blessing.

'Theirs is the kingdom of heaven'

And the Saviour adds more - *'Theirs is the kingdom of heaven'*. What a shock would be felt throughout the crowd. The kingdom could be enjoyed in the present; it could be entered now! The people heard that they did not need to wait until the physical kingdom was set up: the King was here and this privilege of enjoying the kingdom was to those who were righteous and humble minded (poor in spirit) – verse 3.

---

[154]Matthew 27. 35

[155]John 19. 7: 'The Jews answered him, We have a law, and by our law he ought to die, because he made himself the Son of God.'

[156]Matthew 27. 18: 'For he knew that for envy they had delivered him.'

[157]Horatius Bonar: 'Go, labour on; spend, and be spent.'

[158]Psalm 23. 3

For many, Christianity has become socially acceptable. They have camouflaged themselves to be no different from anyone else. They think that they can enjoy all the world's pleasures and still be a Christian. This is not possible[159]. A true follower of Christ is expected to be like his Master, and living a holy life is costly and will bring persecution. There is not another kingdom; there is not another way. Darkness will hate light; sin will oppose righteousness. If at this moment you are feeling pressurised or even know persecution for Christ, then take heart – even in the most difficult of days, you are greatly blessed. Peter could add: *'if you suffer for righteousness' sake, happy are ye'*[160].

[159]Matthew 6. 24: 'No man can serve two masters: for either he will hate the one, and love the other; or else he will hold to the one, and despise the other. Ye cannot serve God and mammon.'

James 4. 4: 'Ye adulterers and adulteresses, know ye not that the friendship of the world is enmity with God? whosoever therefore will be a friend of the world is the enemy of God.'

[160]1 Peter 3. 14: 'But and if ye suffer for righteousness' sake, happy are ye: and be not afraid of their terror, neither be troubled.'

1 Peter 4. 12-16: 'Beloved, think it not strange concerning the fiery trial which is to try you, as though some strange thing happened unto you: But rejoice, inasmuch as ye are partakers of Christ's sufferings; that, when his glory shall be revealed, ye may be glad also with exceeding joy. If ye be reproached for the name of Christ, happy are ye; for the spirit of glory and of God resteth upon you: on their part he is evil spoken of, but on your part he is glorified. But let none of you suffer as a murderer, or as a thief, or as an evildoer, or as a busybody in other men's matters. Yet if any man suffer as a Christian, let him not be ashamed; but let him glorify God on this behalf.'

Lesson

We can take great encouragement from the fact that
suffering for righteousness'
sake will result in reigning with
Christ. What does practical
righteousness look like in my
life? Do I bear reproach for this?

Yea, and all that will live godly in Christ
Jesus shall suffer persecution.

2 Timothy 3.12

Yet if any man suffer as a Christian, let
him not be ashamed.

1 Peter 4.16

Notes

Blessed are ye, when men shall revile you, and persecute you, and shall say all manner of evil against you falsely, for my sake. Rejoice, and be exceeding glad: for great is your reward in heaven: for so persecuted they the prophets which were before you. (Matthew 5.11-12)

The blessing for those who are slandered for Christ

𝒯his final and ninth beatitude from the Lord is not a repeat of the eighth blessing. Although connected with the previous beatitude it is particularly associated with persecution for the sake of Christ: *'for my sake'*. Being persecuted for the Name of Christ i.e. being persecuted for His honour and glory is a theme in Matthew; seven times over we find the Saviour warning that His disciples should anticipate this.[161] It is in that Name we were saved[162]. It is into that Name believers are baptised[163] and it is into that Name that disciples gather together taking no other Name, no sectarian title[164].

---

[161]Matthew 10.18: 'And ye shall be brought before governors and kings for my sake, for a testimony against them and the Gentiles';
Matthew 10.22: 'And ye shall be hated of all men for my name's sake: but he that endureth to the end shall be saved.'
Matthew 10.39: 'He that findeth his life shall lose it: and he that loseth his life for my sake shall find it.'
Matthew 16.25: 'For whosoever will save his life shall lose it: and whosoever will lose his life for my sake shall find it.'

The sneer, the personal insult, the public slander or false accusation can only be endured if it is for His sake. If it is for anyone else's Name – including our own - it would be unbearable. It is only because we have come to love the Man who died for us on the centre cross and rose again that we have any desire to endure the persecution. It is only because of Him and through His grace and power that these extreme experiences can be borne at all. Furthermore, it is also only when we consider these things from an eternal standpoint that we can ever reach the point of calling the experience of being "reviled" for Christ a "blessing".

Our blessed Lord was 'reviled' both from those that passed by[165] and from those crucified with Him[166]. The only good and perfect Man was ridiculed and despised even by those who claimed to follow Moses[167]. Indeed, *'when he was reviled he reviled not again'*[168]. He offered no insult in return to those who abused Him. He *gave His back to the smiters*, He gave *His cheek to those who plucked off the hair*, He *hid not His face from shame and spitting*[169]. He opened His hand to receive the nail. He felt every insult and experienced the searing pain of every crack of the whip, but He never failed; nor

Matthew 19.29: 'And every one that hath forsaken houses, or brethren, or sisters, or father, or mother, or wife, or children, or lands, for my name's sake, shall receive an hundredfold, and shall inherit everlasting life.'

Matthew 24.9: 'Then shall they deliver you up to be afflicted, and shall kill you: and ye shall be hated of all nations for my name's sake.'

[162]Acts 4.12: 'Neither is there salvation in any other: for there is none other name under heaven given among men, whereby we must be saved.'

[163]Matthew 28.19: 'Go ye therefore, and teach all nations, baptizing them in the name of the Father, and of the Son, and of the Holy Ghost';

Acts 19.5: 'When they heard this, they were baptized in the name of the Lord Jesus.'

could He fail[170]. Unlike all other men He had no cracking point. He suffered for the glory of God[171] and out of love to us[172].

We can never enter into the sufferings of Christ for sin, but we can suffer for His Name's sake. Paul wrote, *'being reviled, we bless; being persecuted, we suffer it; being defamed, we intreat'*[173]. This was high ground and an experience he called being *'fools for Christ's sake'*[174] in the eyes of the world. As an intellectual, being considered a fool must have hurt Paul more deeply than any stripes he received from a Roman whip.

Slander can hurt deeply. Being falsely accused (*'say all manner of evil against you falsely'*) is very difficult to bear. Peter qualifies this in First Peter 4 and verse 15 saying we should not allow ourselves to be condemned as a murderer or as a thief. However, he does say if we suffer *'for the name of Christ, happy are ye'*[175]. The Lord was falsely accused of having "*a demon*"[176]; Paul was falsely accused of being *'a mover of sedition'*[177]. Christianity was never considered an easy path. Love for Christ will bring us contempt from the world but pleasure to God.

We are not the first to suffer for Him. The Saviour said, *'they persecuted the prophets which were before you'*. Reading about the

[164]Matthew 18.20: 'For where two or three are gathered together in my name, there am I in the midst of them.'

[165]Matthew 27.39: 'And they that passed by reviled him, wagging their heads.'

[166]Mark 15.32: 'Let Christ the King of Israel descend now from the cross, that we may see and believe. And they that were crucified with him reviled him.'

[167]John 9.28: 'Then they reviled him, and said, Thou art his disciple; but we are Moses' disciples.'

[168]1 Peter 2.23

experiences of God's servants in the Scriptures can help us to endure the Christian pathway today. The ultimate encouragement is Christ Himself: *'Christ also suffered for us, leaving us an example that ye should follow his steps'*. Read also John 13.38[178]; Mark 10.29[179]; Philippians 1.29[180]; Revelation 2.3[181].

It was the Lord Jesus who spoke of disciples gathering to His Name alone. He never established any system in the Upper Room. The Hebrew writer says that we stand *outside the camp* with Him and *'Here we have no continuing city'*[182] i.e. centre of administration. The simplicity of the place of the Name will result in reproach. Human organisations and systems have been built up over the centuries establishing sectarian titles and rules which have affected many true believers. Remember that the reproach of being associated with a small assembly, with nothing to commend it in the eyes of the world or Christendom, is suffering for 'His Name's sake.

[169]Isaiah 50.6

[170]Isaiah 42.4: 'He shall not fail nor be discouraged, till he have set judgment in the earth: and the isles shall wait for his law'

[171]Hebrews 10.5-10: 'Wherefore when he cometh into the world, he saith, Sacrifice and offering thou wouldest not, but a body hast thou prepared me: In burnt offerings and sacrifices for sin thou hast had no pleasure. Then said I, Lo, I come (in the volume of the book it is written of me,) to do thy will, O God. Above when he said, Sacrifice and offering and burnt offerings and offering for sin thou wouldest not, neither hadst pleasure therein; which are offered by the law; Then said he, Lo, I come to do thy will, O God. He taketh away the first, that he may establish the second. By the which will we are sanctified through the offering of the body of Jesus Christ once for all.'

1 Peter 2.23: 'Who, when he was reviled, reviled not again; when he suffered, he threatened not; but committed himself to him that judgeth righteously.'

'Great is your reward in Heaven.'

What a statement! Our blessed Lord was clearly teaching His people that they would one day go to heaven – unlike some false cult teaching today which insists that believers will be blessed only on earth. In another place He called it *'the Father's House'*[183] and another place, *'Paradise'*[184]. Paul described it as *'present with the Lord'*[185]. Every Christian should take great comfort from the hope of Heaven, to be with Christ forever.

In this beatitude the Lord Jesus was also teaching that there would be rewards in heaven for those who suffered for His sake. The Lord taught about open rewards for those who sacrificed in secret[186], prayed in private[187], fasted with fear to God alone[188], and supported struggling disciples with even a sip of water[189]. The third chapter of First Corinthians explains that rewards at the judgment seat of Christ will also be given for all acts of love and truth for the Name of Christ in the assembly of God's people. The

---

[172]1 Peter 2.21, 24: 'For even hereunto were ye called: because Christ also suffered for us, leaving us an example, that ye should follow his steps:… Who his own self bare our sins in his own body on the tree, that we, being dead to sins, should live unto righteousness: by whose stripes ye were healed.'

[173]1 Corinthians 4.12-13

[174]1 Corinthians 4.10

[175]1 Peter 4.14

[176]John 8.48: 'Then answered the Jews, and said unto him, Say we not well that thou art a Samaritan, and hast a devil?'

[177]Acts 24.5

[178]John 13.38: 'Jesus answered him, Wilt thou lay down thy life for my sake? Verily, verily, I say unto thee, The cock shall not crow, till thou hast denied me thrice.'

[179]Mark 19.29-30: 'And Jesus answered and said, Verily I say unto you,

fact that there will be rewards for our works for Christ[190] should encourage us and motivate us to live for the other world. Surely, we can say with the apostle Paul, '*I reckon that the sufferings of this present time are not worthy to be compared with the glory which shall be revealed in us*'[191].

In these nine beatitudes the Lord Jesus blesses those who exhibit self-emptied lives, and those who sorrow for the conditions that the people of God are living in, longing for better days.

He blesses those who are striving for righteousness and He counts them happy who show sympathy and mercy to others and are marked by sanctity and true holiness in their lives.

He regards as sons those who go out of their way to make peace with others and create harmony amongst God's people. In His final blessings He promises rewards to those who are suffering for righteousness and are reproached and being slandered for His Name's sake.

All believers will bow their head in worship to Him saying, '*He is worthy*'.

There is no man that hath left house, or brethren, or sisters, or father, or mother, or wife, or children, or lands, for my sake, and the gospel's, But he shall receive an hundredfold now in this time, houses, and brethren, and sisters, and mothers, and children, and lands, with persecutions; and in the world to come eternal life.'

[180]Philippians 1.29: 'For unto you it is given in the behalf of Christ, not only to believe on him, but also to suffer for his sake.'

[181]Revelation 2.3: 'And hast borne, and hast patience, and for my name's sake hast laboured, and hast not fainted.'

[182]Hebrews 13.14

[183]John 14.1-3: 'Let not your heart be troubled: ye believe in God, believe also in me. In my Father's house are many mansions: if it were not so, I would have told you. I go to prepare a place for you. And if I go and prepare a place for you, I will come again, and receive you unto myself; that where I am, there ye may be also.'

[184]Luke 23.43: 'And Jesus said unto him, Verily I say unto thee, To day shalt thou be with me in paradise.'

[185]2 Corinthians 5.8: 'We are confident, I say, and willing rather to be absent from the body, and to be present with the Lord.'

[186]Matthew 6.4: 'That thine alms may be in secret: and thy Father which seeth in secret himself shall reward thee openly.'

[187]Matthew 6.6: 'But thou, when thou prayest, enter into thy closet, and when thou hast shut thy door, pray to thy Father which is in secret; and thy Father which seeth in secret shall reward thee openly.'

[188]Matthew 6.16-18: 'Moreover when ye fast, be not, as the hypocrites, of a sad countenance: for they disfigure their faces, that they may appear unto men to fast. Verily I say unto you, They have their reward.

But thou, when thou fastest, anoint thine head, and wash thy face; That thou appear not unto men to fast, but unto thy Father which is in secret: and thy Father, which seeth in secret, shall reward thee openly.'

[189]Matthew 10.42: 'And whosoever shall give to drink unto one of these little ones a cup of cold water only in the name of a disciple, verily I say unto you, he shall in no wise lose his reward.'

[190]Matthew 16.27 'For the Son of man shall come in the glory of his Father with his angels; and then he shall reward every man according to his works.'

[191]Romans 8.18

Lesson

We can take great encouragement from the fact that
suffering for righteousness'
sake will result in reigning with
Christ. What does practical
righteousness look like in my
life? Do I bear reproach for this?

For I will shew him how great things he
must suffer for my name's sake.

Acts 9.16

Notes

Characteristics

Each beatitude describes a feature that should mark the believer:

	Blessed are...	or those who are:
1	the poor in spirit	*self-emptied*
2	they that mourn	*sorrowful*
3	the meek	*self-restrained*
4	they which do hunger and thirst after righteousness	*striving for righteousness*
5	the merciful	*sympathetic*
6	the pure in heart	*sanctified*
7	the peacemakers	*serene*
8	they which are persecuted for righteousness' sake	*suffering*
9	ye when men shall revile you, and persecute you, and shall say all manner of evil against you falsely, for my sake	*slandered*

Outcomes

Each beatitude also describes the outcome for the believer if these characteristics are displayed in them.

For....

1	**theirs is the kingdom of heaven**	*privilege*
2	**they shall be comforted**	*protection*
3	**they shall inherit the earth**	*possession*
4	**they shall be filled**	*provision*
5	**they shall obtain mercy**	*pitied*
6	**they shall see God**	*pre-eminence*
7	**they shall be called the children of God**	*position*
8	**theirs is the kingdom of heaven**	*privilege*
9	**Rejoice, and be exceeding glad: for great is your reward in heaven: for so persecuted they the prophets which were before you**	*prize*

Appendix 1: Eight beatitudes of Luke

Luke 6.20 And he lifted up his eyes on his disciples, and said, Blessed be ye poor: for yours is the kingdom of God.

Luke 6.21 Blessed are ye that hunger now: for ye shall be filled. Blessed are ye that weep now: for ye shall laugh.

Luke 6.22 Blessed are ye, when men shall hate you, and when they shall separate you from their company, and shall reproach you, and cast out your name as evil, for the Son of man's sake.

Luke 10.23   And he turned him unto his disciples, and said privately, Blessed are the eyes which see the things that ye see:

Luke 11.28 But he said, Yea rather, blessed are they that hear the word of God, and keep it.

Luke 12.37 Blessed are those servants, whom the lord when he cometh shall find watching: verily I say unto you, that he shall gird himself, and make them to sit down to meat, and will come forth and serve them.

Luke 12.38 And if he shall come in the second watch, or come in the third watch, and find them so, blessed are those servants.

Luke 23.29 For, behold, the days are coming, in the which they shall say, Blessed are the barren, and the wombs that never bare, and the paps which never gave suck.

Appendix 2: Seven Beatitudes of Revelation

Rev 1.3 Blessed is he that readeth, and they that hear the words of this prophecy, and keep those things which are written therein: for the time is at hand.

Rev 14.13 And I heard a voice from heaven saying unto me, Write, Blessed are the dead which die in the Lord from henceforth: Yea, saith the Spirit, that they may rest from their labours; and their works do follow them.

Rev 16.15 Behold, I come as a thief. Blessed is he that watcheth, and keepeth his garments, lest he walk naked, and they see his shame.

Rev 19.9 And he saith unto me, Write, Blessed are they which are called unto the marriage supper of the Lamb. And he saith unto me, These are the true sayings of God.

Rev 20.6 Blessed and holy is he that hath part in the first resurrection: on such the second death hath no power, but they shall be priests of God and of Christ, and shall reign with him a thousand years.

Rev 22.7 Behold, I come quickly: blessed is he that keepeth the sayings of the prophecy of this book.

Rev 22.14 Blessed are they that do his commandments, that they may have right to the tree of life, and may enter in through the gates into the city.

Appendix 3: Psalm beatitudes (14 verses)

Psalm 2.12 Kiss the Son, lest he be angry, and ye perish from the way, when his wrath is kindled but a little. Blessed are all they that put their trust in him.

Psalm 32.1-2   Blessed is he whose transgression is forgiven, whose sin is covered. Blessed is the man unto whom the LORD imputeth not iniquity, and in whose spirit there is no guile.

Psalm 34.8 O taste and see that the LORD is good: blessed is the man that trusteth in him.

Psalm 40.4 Blessed is that man that maketh the LORD his trust, and respecteth not the proud, nor such as turn aside to lies.

Psalm 41.1 Blessed is he that considereth the poor: the LORD will deliver him in time of trouble.

Psalm 65.4 Blessed is the man whom thou choosest, and causest to approach unto thee, that he may dwell in thy courts: we shall be satisfied with the goodness of thy house, even of thy holy temple.

Psalm 84.4 Blessed are they that dwell in thy house: they will be still praising thee. Selah.

Psalm 84.5 Blessed is the man whose strength is in thee; in whose heart are the ways of them.

Psalm 94.12 Blessed is the man whom thou chastenest, O LORD, and teachest him out of thy law;

Psalm 106.3 Blessed are they that keep judgment, and he that doeth righteousness at all times.

Psalm 112.1 Praise ye the LORD. Blessed is the man that feareth the LORD, that delighteth greatly in his commandments.

Psalm 119.1 Blessed are the undefiled in the way, who walk in the law of the LORD.

Psalm 119.2 Blessed are they that keep his testimonies, and that seek him with the whole heart.

Psalm 128.1 Blessed is every one that feareth the LORD; that walketh in his ways.

The Nine Beatitudes

The Nine Beatitudes